The Zimbabwe P

Step into the rich and vibrant
with "The Zimbabwe Pantry,"
book that captures the essenc
heritage. Embark on a mouthw
heart of Zimbabwe, exploring a of traditional
flavours and time-honoured recipes passed down through
generations.

Within the pages of "The Zimbabwe Pantry," you will discover an array of sumptuous dishes that showcase the country's diverse cultural influences and indigenous ingredients. From the sizzling aroma of savoury Braai barbecue to the comforting warmth of Nyama stews, each recipe is lovingly curated to transport you to the heart of Zimbabwean households, where food is more than sustenance – it's a celebration of life, family, and community.

Whether you are a seasoned chef looking to expand your culinary repertoire or a curious food enthusiast eager to explore new tastes, "The Zimbabwe Pantry" offers an inviting and accessible collection of recipes that cater to all skill levels.

Beyond its delectable recipes, "The Zimbabwe Pantry" delves into the cultural significance of food in Zimbabwe, providing a deeper understanding of the country's traditions and customs. It's a celebration of the country's rich history, told through the medium of delicious cuisine that reflects the harmony between nature and the Zimbabwean way of life.

So, open the pages of "The Zimbabwe Pantry" and embark on an unforgettable gastronomic adventure. Whether you seek to recreate nostalgic flavours or embrace the allure of a distant land, this cookbook will undoubtedly become a cherished addition to your kitchen, infusing your meals with the warmth and soul of Zimbabwe.

Index

1. Sadza: A staple food made from finely ground maize meal, served with various relishes.
2. Nyama Choma: Grilled or roasted meat, often served with vegetables and sauces.
3. Muriwo Unedovi: Cooked leafy greens, typically prepared with groundnut butter.
4. Dovi: A peanut butter stew made with chicken or beef and served with sadza.
5. Huku NeDovi: Chicken cooked in peanut butter sauce.
6. Matemba: Dried fish stewed with tomatoes, onions, and spices.
7. Bota: Traditional porridge made from sorghum or millet.
8. Mazondo: Ox trotters or cow hooves cooked until tender in a flavourful stew.
9. Muboora: Pumpkin leaves cooked with peanut butter and other vegetables.
10. Mopane Worms: Dried and rehydrated caterpillars, often sautéed with onions and tomatoes.
11. Mutakura: Traditional Zimbabwean relish made from baobab leaves.
12. Chikafu Chembudzi: Goat meat stew seasoned with spices and tomatoes.
13. Chingwa: Wild fruits, particularly the baobab fruit, often used in sauces or porridge.
14. Dovi Na Banana: A unique dish combining peanut butter stew with bananas.
15. Madora: Flying ants, a seasonal delicacy often enjoyed fried or in stews.
16. Maguru/Mudende: Beef or goat tripe, usually cooked until tender in a spicy sauce.
17. Masawu: Small dried fish often used to add flavour to various dishes.
18. Chibage Chaunobhobho: Roasted corn on the cob, popular street food.
19. Dochi: Cooked pumpkin with groundnut butter and spices.
20. Mufushwa: Fermented milk, similar to yogurt, served as a beverage or dessert.

21. Nhingwa: Roasted peanuts, a common snack in Zimbabwe.
22. Gurundoro: Traditional Zimbabwean popcorn.
23. Rupiza: Groundnut flour used in various dishes and as a thickener for stews.
24. Bohobe: Sorghum and maize drink often consumed at special occasions.
25. Chikanda: A dessert made from groundnuts and wild orchid tubers.
26. Chakalaka: A spicy vegetable relish that complements many dishes.
27. Chingondora: A dish made from pumpkin flowers and groundnut butter.
28. Mapopo Candy: Candied or dried guava fruit.
29. Dobi: Traditional Zimbabwean greens similar to spinach.
30. Chikwata: A sweet and sour sauce made from tamarind fruit, used as a dip or marinade.

These traditional Zimbabwean recipes showcase the country's unique flavours and ingredients, reflecting the cultural diversity and culinary creativity of the Zimbabwean people.

Sadza - Zimbabwean Cornmeal Porridge

Sadza is the quintessential staple food of Zimbabwe, enjoyed by many as a comforting and filling dish. Made from finely ground maize meal, this cornmeal porridge is typically served with an array of delicious relishes. The process of making Sadza requires patience and attention, as achieving the perfect consistency is crucial to its success. So, let's dive into this traditional recipe step by step:

Ingredients:
2 cups white maize meal (cornmeal)
4 cups water
A pinch of salt (optional)
Butter or cooking oil (for serving)

Instructions:
Preparing the Maize Meal:
In a large bowl, add the maize meal and a pinch of salt (if using).
Gradually add 2 cups of water while stirring continuously to create a smooth paste. This initial mixture is known as "dobi."
Set the remaining 2 cups of water aside for later use.

Cooking the Sadza:
Pour the dobi mixture into a large, heavy-bottomed pot or cooking pot.
Place the pot over medium heat and add the remaining 2 cups of water gradually while stirring constantly to avoid lumps.

Stirring and Cooking:
Using a wooden spoon or Sadza stick, stir the mixture vigorously to break up any lumps and create a smooth consistency.
Continue stirring the mixture as it cooks to prevent it from sticking to the bottom of the pot.

Achieving the Right Consistency:
As the Sadza cooks, it will thicken. Keep stirring until it reaches a stiff, smooth consistency similar to thick mashed potatoes.
Adjust the heat as needed to avoid burning and maintain a steady cooking pace.

The "Bubbling" Phase:
At this point, the Sadza should be bubbling and thickening further.
Reduce the heat to low, cover the pot with a lid, and let it simmer for about 5-10 minutes. This helps to cook the maize meal thoroughly.

Shaping the Sadza:
To shape the Sadza traditionally, wet a bowl or a small container with water.
Scoop out portions of the cooked Sadza and press them into the wet container to mould them into individual portions.

Serving:
Once shaped, carefully invert the container onto a serving plate to release the molded Sadza.

Traditionally, Sadza is served with relishes such as stewed meat, vegetables, or sauces.

Add a dollop of butter or drizzle some cooking oil over the Sadza before serving, enhancing its flavour and texture.

Enjoy your hearty and flavourful Sadza, a beloved Zimbabwean classic that embodies the soul of the nation's cuisine!

Nyama Choma - Zimbabwean Grilled or Roasted Meat

Nyama Choma is a beloved dish in Zimbabwe, showcasing the country's love for flavourful grilled or roasted meat. Whether enjoyed at family gatherings, social events, or as a delicious weekend treat, Nyama Choma is a dish that brings people together. Here's a step-by-step guide to preparing this mouthwatering delicacy:

Ingredients:

1kg of beef, goat, or chicken (choose your preferred meat cut, such as ribs, steaks, or skewers)
2 tablespoons vegetable oil
2 cloves of garlic, minced
1-inch piece of fresh ginger, grated
1 tablespoon paprika
1 teaspoon ground cumin
1 teaspoon ground coriander
1 teaspoon salt (adjust to taste)
1/2 teaspoon freshly ground black pepper
Lemon or lime wedges (for serving)

Instructions:

Marinating the Meat:
In a large mixing bowl, combine vegetable oil, minced garlic, grated ginger, paprika, ground cumin, ground coriander, salt, and black pepper. Mix well to create a flavourful marinade.
Add the meat pieces to the marinade, ensuring they are thoroughly coated with the spice mixture.
Cover the bowl with plastic wrap or a lid and refrigerate for at least 2 hours (or preferably overnight) to allow the flavours to penetrate the meat.

Preparing the Grill or Oven:
If using a grill, preheat it to medium-high heat. If using an oven, preheat it to 180°C.

Grilling or Roasting the Meat:
If using a grill, remove the marinated meat from the refrigerator and thread it onto skewers (if using smaller cuts) or place larger pieces directly on the grill grates.

Grill the meat on each side until it achieves a nicely charred and caramelized appearance, and the internal temperature reaches your desired level of doneness.

If using an oven, place the marinated meat on a baking sheet lined with foil or a wire rack. Roast the meat in the preheated oven until cooked to your preferred level (usually 20-30 minutes, depending on the cut and thickness).

Resting the Meat:
Once the Nyama Choma is cooked, remove it from the grill or oven and let it rest for a few minutes before serving. This allows the juices to redistribute, ensuring a moist and flavourful final dish.

Serving:
Transfer the Nyama Choma to a serving platter and garnish with lemon or lime wedges for an extra burst of citrusy flavour.

Nyama Choma is typically served with assorted vegetables, such as sliced tomatoes, cucumbers, and onions.

You can also serve it with various dipping sauces or chutneys for added taste and variety.

Enjoy the succulent and smoky delights of Nyama Choma, a true taste of Zimbabwe's passion for grilled or roasted meat!

Muriwo Unedovi - Zimbabwean Leafy Greens with Groundnut Butter

Muriwo Unedovi is a delightful Zimbabwean dish that highlights the natural flavours of leafy greens and the richness of groundnut butter (peanut butter). This nutritious and satisfying side dish is a favourite accompaniment to many Zimbabwean meals. Let's explore how to prepare Muriwo Unedovi step by step:

Ingredients:

1 bunch of leafy greens (spinach, collard greens, or kale), washed and chopped
1 medium onion, finely chopped
2 cloves of garlic, minced
2 tablespoons vegetable oil
1/2 cup groundnut butter (smooth or chunky)
1 cup vegetable or chicken broth (or water)
Salt and pepper to taste

Instructions:
Preparing the Leafy Greens:
Wash the leafy greens thoroughly under running water to remove any dirt or grit. Drain them in a colander and chop them into bite-sized pieces.

Sautéing the Aromatics:
In a large, deep fry pan or saucepan, heat the vegetable oil over medium heat.
Add the finely chopped onions and minced garlic to the hot oil. Sauté until the onions become translucent and fragrant, about 2-3 minutes.

Cooking the Leafy Greens:
Add the chopped leafy greens to the fry pan, stirring well to combine them with the sautéed onions and garlic.

Let the greens cook down for a few minutes until they wilt and reduce in volume.

Adding the Groundnut Butter:
Once the greens are wilted, add the groundnut butter (peanut butter) to the fry pan.
Mix the groundnut butter with the greens until it coats them evenly.

Adding Broth (or Water) and Seasoning:
Pour in the vegetable or chicken broth (or water) to the fry pan, stirring gently to create a creamy sauce with the groundnut butter.
Season the dish with salt and pepper to taste. Remember, the groundnut butter already adds some nuttiness and saltiness, so adjust the seasoning accordingly.

Simmering and Thickening:
Reduce the heat to low, cover the fry pan with a lid, and let the Muriwo Unedovi simmer gently for about 10-15 minutes.
The dish will thicken slightly, and the flavours will meld together beautifully during this time.

Serving:
Once the Muriwo Unedovi is cooked to your desired consistency, remove it from the heat.

Serve the dish as a delightful accompaniment to Sadza (cornmeal porridge) or other Zimbabwean main dishes.

Enjoy the goodness of Muriwo Unedovi, a delectable blend of leafy greens and creamy groundnut butter that exemplifies the wholesome simplicity of Zimbabwean cuisine!

Dovi - Zimbabwean Peanut Butter Stew with Chicken (or Beef)

Dovi is a comforting and flavourful peanut butter stew that is a true delight in Zimbabwean cuisine. This hearty dish combines the richness of peanut butter with tender chicken (or beef) to create a creamy and satisfying stew. Traditionally served with Sadza (cornmeal porridge), Dovi is a favourite among families and friends. Let's learn how to make this delicious Zimbabwean dish step by step:

Ingredients:
1 kg chicken pieces (or beef, cut into bite-sized chunks)
1 large onion, finely chopped
2 cloves of garlic, minced
1-inch piece of fresh ginger, grated
2 tablespoons vegetable oil
1 cup smooth peanut butter
2 large tomatoes, chopped
2 cups chicken broth (or water)
1 cup chopped mixed vegetables (carrots, capsicums, and/or green beans)
Salt and pepper to taste
Chopped fresh cilantro or parsley (for garnish)
Sadza (cornmeal porridge) for serving

Instructions:
Browning the Meat:
In a large, heavy-bottomed pot or Dutch oven, heat the vegetable oil over medium-high heat.
Add the chicken pieces (or beef chunks) to the hot oil and brown them on all sides. Remove the browned meat from the pot and set it aside.

Sautéing the Aromatics:
In the same pot, add the finely chopped onions and sauté until they become translucent, about 2-3 minutes.
Stir in the minced garlic and grated ginger, and cook for an additional minute until aromatic.

Creating the Stew Base:
Return the browned meat to the pot with the sautéed aromatics.
Add the smooth peanut butter to the pot, stirring it well to coat the meat and onions.

Adding Tomatoes and Broth (or Water):
Incorporate the chopped tomatoes into the stew, allowing them to break down and release their juices.
Pour in the chicken broth (or water) to the pot, stirring to combine all the ingredients.

Simmering the Stew:
Bring the Dovi to a gentle simmer, then cover the pot with a lid and let it cook over low to medium heat for about 30-40 minutes (or longer for beef), or until the meat is tender and cooked through.

Adding Vegetables and Seasoning:
Add the chopped mixed vegetables to the stew, stirring them in to cook until tender-crisp.
Season the Dovi with salt and pepper to taste, adjusting the flavours according to your preference.

Serving:
Once the Dovi is cooked to perfection, remove the pot from the heat.
Garnish the stew with chopped fresh cilantro or parsley for a burst of freshness.

Serve the Dovi hot alongside Sadza, allowing the creamy peanut butter stew to complement the comforting cornmeal porridge.

Enjoy the hearty and soul-warming flavours of Dovi, a traditional Zimbabwean dish that brings together the rich taste of peanut butter and tender meat in a truly delightful stew.

Huku NeDovi - Zimbabwean Chicken in Peanut Butter Sauce

Huku NeDovi is a delectable Zimbabwean dish that features tender chicken pieces cooked in a luscious and creamy peanut butter sauce. This flavourful and hearty stew is a true crowd-pleaser, often served with Sadza (cornmeal porridge) or rice for a complete and satisfying meal. Let's dive into the step-by-step guide to making this mouthwatering Zimbabwean classic:

Ingredients:

1 kg chicken pieces (skin-on, bone-in, or boneless, based on preference)
1 large onion, finely chopped
2 cloves of garlic, minced
1-inch piece of fresh ginger, grated
2 tablespoons vegetable oil
1 cup smooth peanut butter
2 large tomatoes, chopped
2 cups chicken broth (or water)
1 cup mixed vegetables (carrots, capsicums, and/or green beans)
1 tablespoon curry powder (optional, for added flavour)
Salt and pepper to taste
Chopped fresh cilantro or parsley (for garnish)
Sadza (cornmeal porridge) or rice for serving

Instructions:

Sautéing the Aromatics:
In a large, heavy-bottomed pot or Dutch oven, heat the vegetable oil over medium-high heat.
Add the finely chopped onions and sauté until they become translucent, about 2-3 minutes.
Stir in the minced garlic and grated ginger, and cook for an additional minute until aromatic.

Browning the Chicken:
Add the chicken pieces to the pot with the sautéed aromatics.

Brown the chicken on all sides to seal in the juices and enhance the flavours. Remove the browned chicken from the pot and set it aside.

Preparing the Peanut Butter Sauce:
In the same pot, reduce the heat to medium and add the smooth peanut butter.
Stir the peanut butter to soften it and create a smooth consistency.

Adding Tomatoes and Broth (or Water):
Incorporate the chopped tomatoes into the peanut butter sauce, stirring well to combine.
Pour in the chicken broth (or water) to the pot, stirring continuously to create a creamy sauce.

Simmering the Chicken in the Peanut Butter Sauce:Return the browned chicken to the pot, making sure it is submerged in the peanut butter sauce.
If using curry powder for added flavour, sprinkle it over the chicken and sauce at this stage.
Bring the mixture to a gentle simmer, then cover the pot with a lid.

Cooking the Chicken:

Let the Huku NeDovi simmer over low to medium heat for about 30-40 minutes (or longer, depending on the size of the chicken pieces), or until the chicken is tender and thoroughly cooked.

Adding Vegetables and Seasoning:
Add the mixed vegetables to the pot, stirring them into the sauce.
Season the dish with salt and pepper to taste, adjusting the flavours according to your preference.

Serving:
Once the Huku NeDovi is cooked to perfection, remove the pot from the heat.
Garnish the dish with chopped fresh cilantro or parsley for a burst of freshness and vibrant colour.
Serve the Huku NeDovi hot, alongside Sadza or rice, allowing the creamy peanut butter sauce to meld with the succulent chicken for a truly delightful meal.

Enjoy the rich and creamy goodness of Huku NeDovi, a classic Zimbabwean dish that showcases the exquisite combination of chicken and peanut butter sauce!

Matemba - Zimbabwean Dried Fish Stew

Matemba is a delightful Zimbabwean dish that features dried fish stewed with a flavourful combination of tomatoes, onions, and spices. This hearty and savoury stew is a culinary delight that showcases the unique taste of dried fish. Let's explore how to prepare this traditional Zimbabwean recipe step by step:

Ingredients:
250g dried fish (tilapia, bream, or any dried fish of your choice)
2 large tomatoes, chopped
1 large onion, finely chopped
2 cloves of garlic, minced
1-inch piece of fresh ginger, grated
2 tablespoons vegetable oil
1 teaspoon ground paprika
1 teaspoon ground cumin
1 teaspoon ground coriander
1/2 teaspoon ground turmeric
1/2 teaspoon ground black pepper
Salt to taste
Chopped fresh cilantro or parsley (for garnish)
Cooked rice or Sadza (cornmeal porridge) for serving

Instructions:
Preparing the Dried Fish:
Rinse the dried fish thoroughly under cold running water to remove excess salt and any impurities.
Place the dried fish in a bowl of water and soak it for at least 1 hour (or longer if needed) to rehydrate. Change the water a few times during the soaking process.

Sautéing the Aromatics:
In a large, deep fry pan or saucepan, heat the vegetable oil over medium heat.
Add the finely chopped onions and sauté until they become translucent, about 2-3 minutes.

Stir in the minced garlic and grated ginger, and cook for an additional minute until aromatic.

Adding Tomatoes and Spices:
Incorporate the chopped tomatoes into the sautéed aromatics, stirring well to combine.
Add ground paprika, ground cumin, ground coriander, ground turmeric, and ground black pepper to the tomato mixture. Mix the spices with the tomatoes and onions to create a flavourful base for the stew.

Stewing the Dried Fish:
Drain the rehydrated dried fish and pat it dry with paper towels.
Add the dried fish to the tomato and spice mixture in the fry pan, gently nestling the fish into the stew.

Simmering the Stew:
Pour enough water into the fry pan to just cover the dried fish and tomato mixture.
Bring the stew to a gentle simmer, then cover the fry pan with a lid.

Cooking the Stew:
Let the Matemba simmer over low heat for about 20-30 minutes, allowing the flavours to meld together and the fish to become tender.

Adjusting Seasoning and Serving:
Taste the stew and add salt if needed, adjusting the seasoning to your preference.
Once the Matemba is cooked to perfection, remove the fry pan from the heat.
Garnish the dish with chopped fresh cilantro or parsley for a burst of freshness.

Serve the Matemba hot, accompanied by cooked rice or Sadza, allowing the delectable dried fish stew to be the star of the meal.

Enjoy the rich and savoury flavours of Matemba, a traditional Zimbabwean delicacy that brings the delightful taste of dried fish to the forefront of your palate!

Bota - Zimbabwean Sorghum or Millet Porridge

Bota is a beloved Zimbabwean traditional porridge made from either sorghum or millet. This nutritious and wholesome dish is a staple in many Zimbabwean households, enjoyed as a breakfast or as a comforting snack throughout the day. Let's dive into the step-by-step guide to making this delightful Zimbabwean porridge:

Ingredients:

1 cup sorghum or millet flour
3 cups water
1 cup milk (or coconut milk for a dairy-free option)
2-3 tablespoons sugar (adjust to taste)
Pinch of salt
Ground cinnamon or nutmeg (optional, for added flavour)
Fresh fruits or dried fruit (for topping, optional)

Instructions:
Preparing the Sorghum/Millet Flour:
If you have whole sorghum or millet grains, grind them into a fine flour using a grain mill or a powerful blender. Alternatively, you can purchase sorghum or millet flour from specialty stores or online.

Mixing the Flour and Water:
In a medium-sized saucepan, mix the sorghum or millet flour with 1 cup of water to create a smooth paste, ensuring there are no lumps.

Cooking the Porridge:
Add the remaining 2 cups of water to the saucepan, stirring well to combine the flour mixture with the water.
Place the saucepan over medium heat and bring the mixture to a gentle boil, stirring frequently to prevent sticking or burning.

Simmering and Thickening:
Once the porridge starts to boil, reduce the heat to low and let it simmer for about 15-20 minutes, or until it thickens to your desired consistency.
Stir the porridge occasionally during the simmering process to ensure even cooking.

Adding Milk and Sweetener:
Pour in the milk (or coconut milk) to the porridge, stirring it in to create a creamy texture.
Add the sugar and a pinch of salt to the porridge, adjusting the sweetness to your taste preferences.

Enhancing the Flavour (Optional):
For added flavour, you can sprinkle ground cinnamon or nutmeg over the porridge and stir it in. This step is optional but adds a delightful aromatic touch to the Bota.

Serving:
Once the Bota has reached your preferred consistency and flavour, remove the saucepan from the heat.

Serve the warm Bota in bowls, optionally topping it with fresh fruits or dried fruit for added texture and sweetness.

Enjoy the comforting and nourishing taste of Bota, a traditional Zimbabwean porridge made from sorghum or millet, perfect for starting your day or savouring during a relaxing moment!

Mazondo - Zimbabwean Ox Trotters or Cow Hooves Stew

Mazondo is a hearty and flavourful Zimbabwean dish that features ox trotters or cow hooves cooked until tender in a delicious stew. This traditional delicacy is loved for its rich flavours and comforting texture. Let's explore how to prepare Mazondo step by step:

Ingredients:
1 kg ox trotters or cow hooves, cleaned and cut into smaller pieces
1 large onion, finely chopped
2 cloves of garlic, minced
1-inch piece of fresh ginger, grated
2 tablespoons vegetable oil
2 large tomatoes, chopped
1 tablespoon tomato paste
2 cups beef or vegetable broth
1 teaspoon ground paprika
1 teaspoon ground cumin
1 teaspoon ground coriander
1/2 teaspoon ground turmeric
1/2 teaspoon ground black pepper
Salt to taste
Chopped fresh cilantro or parsley (for garnish)
Cooked Sadza (cornmeal porridge) or rice for serving

Instructions:
Preparing the Mazondo:
If using fresh ox trotters or cow hooves, clean them thoroughly under running water to remove any debris or impurities. Cut the larger pieces into smaller, manageable portions.

Sautéing the Aromatics:
In a large, heavy-bottomed pot or Dutch oven, heat the vegetable oil over medium-high heat.
Add the finely chopped onions and sauté until they become translucent, about 2-3 minutes.

Stir in the minced garlic and grated ginger, and cook for an additional minute until aromatic.

Browning the Mazondo:

Add the cleaned ox trotters or cow hooves to the pot with the sautéed aromatics.
Brown the pieces on all sides to enhance the flavours. This step adds depth to the stew.

Adding Tomatoes and Tomato Paste:
Incorporate the chopped tomatoes into the pot, stirring well to combine with the browned Mazondo.
Stir in the tomato paste, distributing it evenly to create a rich tomato base for the stew.

Adding Broth and Spices:
Pour the beef or vegetable broth into the pot, making sure it covers the Mazondo pieces.
Add ground paprika, ground cumin, ground coriander, ground turmeric, and ground black pepper to the pot. Mix the spices with the stew to infuse it with flavours.

Simmering the Stew:
Bring the Mazondo stew to a gentle simmer, then cover the pot with a lid.
Let it cook over low heat for about 2 to 2.5 hours (or longer if needed) until the Mazondo becomes tender and easily falls off the bone.

Adjusting Seasoning and Serving:
Taste the stew and add salt if needed, adjusting the seasoning according to your preference.
Once the Mazondo is cooked to perfection, remove the pot from the heat.

Garnish the dish with chopped fresh cilantro or parsley for a burst of freshness.

Serve the Mazondo hot, accompanied by Sadza or rice, allowing the flavourful stew to meld with the comforting side dish for a satisfying and memorable meal.

Enjoy the rich and tender flavours of Mazondo, a cherished Zimbabwean delicacy that showcases the delightful taste of ox trotters or cow hooves cooked to perfection in a flavourful stew.

Muboora - Zimbabwean Pumpkin Leaves with Peanut Butter

Muboora is a delectable Zimbabwean dish that features pumpkin leaves cooked in a creamy peanut butter sauce, along with other vegetables for added flavour and nutrition. This hearty and nutritious dish is a celebration of Zimbabwe's rich agricultural produce. Let's explore how to prepare Muboora step by step:

Ingredients:

1 large bunch of pumpkin leaves (alternatively, spinach or other leafy greens can be used)
1 large onion, finely chopped
2 cloves of garlic, minced
1-inch piece of fresh ginger, grated
2 tablespoons vegetable oil
1 cup smooth peanut butter
2 large tomatoes, chopped
1 cup mixed vegetables (carrots, capsicums, and/or green beans), chopped
2 cups vegetable broth (or water)
Salt and pepper to taste
Cooked rice or Sadza (cornmeal porridge) for serving

Instructions:

Preparing the Pumpkin Leaves:
Wash the pumpkin leaves thoroughly under running water to remove any dirt or debris.
Separate the leaves from the tough stems and discard the stems.
Chop the pumpkin leaves into smaller pieces.

Sautéing the Aromatics:
In a large, deep fry pan or saucepan, heat the vegetable oil over medium heat.
Add the finely chopped onions and sauté until they become translucent, about 2-3 minutes.

Stir in the minced garlic and grated ginger, and cook for an additional minute until aromatic.

Creating the Peanut Butter Sauce:
Lower the heat to medium-low, then add the smooth peanut butter to the sautéed aromatics.
Stir the peanut butter to soften it and create a smooth and creamy consistency.

Adding Tomatoes and Mixed Vegetables:
Incorporate the chopped tomatoes into the peanut butter sauce, stirring well to combine.
Add the mixed vegetables to the sauce, continuing to stir to mix everything together.

Cooking the Pumpkin Leaves:
Add the chopped pumpkin leaves to the fry pan, stirring them into the peanut butter sauce and vegetables.
Pour the vegetable broth (or water) into the fry pan, ensuring it covers the vegetables and pumpkin leaves.

Simmering the Muboora:
Bring the mixture to a gentle simmer, then cover the fry pan with a lid.
Let the Muboora cook over low heat for about 20-30 minutes, allowing the flavours to meld together and the pumpkin leaves to become tender.

Adjusting Seasoning and Serving:
Taste the Muboora and add salt and pepper to your liking, adjusting the seasoning to your preference.
Once the Muboora is cooked to perfection, remove the fry pan from the heat.

Serving:
Serve the Muboora hot, alongside cooked rice or Sadza, allowing the creamy peanut butter sauce to complement the nutritious pumpkin leaves and vegetables for a satisfying and wholesome meal.

Enjoy the delightful taste of Muboora, a cherished Zimbabwean dish that showcases the flavourful combination of pumpkin leaves cooked in a creamy peanut butter sauce, making it a delightful addition to your dining table!

Mopane Worms - Zimbabwean Sauteed Caterpillars

Mopane worms are a unique and traditional delicacy in Zimbabwe, known for their rich flavour and high nutritional value. In this recipe, we'll learn how to rehydrate dried mopane worms and sauté them with onions and tomatoes for a delicious and savoury dish.

Note: Before preparing this dish, ensure that you have sourced safe-to-eat, dried mopane worms from reputable sources.

Ingredients:
1 cup dried mopane worms
1 large onion, finely chopped
2 large tomatoes, chopped
2 tablespoons vegetable oil
2 cloves of garlic, minced
1 teaspoon ground paprika
1 teaspoon ground cumin
1 teaspoon ground coriander
1/2 teaspoon ground turmeric
Salt and pepper to taste

Instructions:
Rehydrating the Mopane Worms:
Place the dried mopane worms in a bowl of warm water and let them rehydrate for about 15-20 minutes.
After rehydration, drain the mopane worms and squeeze out any excess water.

Sautéing the Aromatics:
In a large fry pan or frying pan, heat the vegetable oil over medium heat.
Add the finely chopped onions and sauté until they become translucent, about 2-3 minutes.
Stir in the minced garlic and cook for an additional minute until aromatic.

Adding the Mopane Worms:
Carefully add the rehydrated mopane worms to the fry pan with the sautéed onions and garlic.
Stir the worms to combine them with the onions, allowing them to absorb the flavours of the aromatics.

Sautéing the Mopane Worms:
Continue sautéing the mopane worms over medium heat for about 5-7 minutes, until they are well-cooked and have a slightly crispy texture.

Adding Tomatoes and Spices:
Add the chopped tomatoes to the fry pan, stirring them in with the mopane worms.
Sprinkle ground paprika, ground cumin, ground coriander, and ground turmeric over the mixture, coating the worms and tomatoes with the spices.

Seasoning and Finalizing:
Season the dish with salt and pepper to taste, adjusting the flavours according to your preference.
Continue cooking the sautéed mopane worms with onions and tomatoes for an additional 2-3 minutes, allowing the flavours to meld together.

Serving:
Once the mopane worms are well-cooked and infused with flavours, remove the fry pan from the heat.

Serve the sautéed mopane worms hot as a unique and traditional Zimbabwean delicacy, perfect as a side dish or even as a main course accompanied by Sadza (cornmeal porridge) or rice.

Enjoy the distinctive and savoury taste of Mopane Worms, a cherished Zimbabwean delicacy that offers a memorable and culturally enriching culinary experience!

Mutakura - Zimbabwean Baobab Leaves Relish

Mutakura is a unique and traditional Zimbabwean relish made from baobab leaves. This flavourful and nutritious dish celebrates the abundant baobab trees found in the region. Let's explore how to prepare Mutakura step by step:

Note: Baobab leaves are typically dried and pounded to make a powdered form called "muboora" in Zimbabwe. If fresh baobab leaves are available, they can be used directly in this recipe.

Ingredients:

1 cup dried baobab leaves (muboora) or 2 cups fresh baobab leaves, washed and chopped
1 large onion, finely chopped
2 large tomatoes, chopped
2 tablespoons vegetable oil
2 cloves of garlic, minced
1 teaspoon ground paprika
1 teaspoon ground cumin
1 teaspoon ground coriander
1/2 teaspoon ground turmeric
Salt and pepper to taste

Instructions:

Preparing the Baobab Leaves:
If using dried baobab leaves (muboora), place them in a bowl of warm water and let them rehydrate for about 15-20 minutes. After rehydration, drain the baobab leaves and squeeze out any excess water. If using fresh baobab leaves, wash them thoroughly and chop them into smaller pieces.

Sautéing the Aromatics:
In a large fry pan or frying pan, heat the vegetable oil over medium heat.
Add the finely chopped onions and sauté until they become translucent, about 2-3 minutes.

Stir in the minced garlic and cook for an additional minute until aromatic.

Adding the Baobab Leaves:
Carefully add the rehydrated baobab leaves or fresh chopped baobab leaves to the fry pan with the sautéed onions and garlic.
Stir the leaves to combine them with the onions, allowing them to absorb the flavours of the aromatics.

Sautéing the Baobab Leaves:
Continue sautéing the baobab leaves over medium heat for about 5-7 minutes, until they are well-cooked and tender.

Adding Tomatoes and Spices:
Add the chopped tomatoes to the fry pan, stirring them in with the baobab leaves.
Sprinkle ground paprika, ground cumin, ground coriander, and ground turmeric over the mixture, coating the leaves and tomatoes with the spices.

Seasoning and Finalizing:
Season the dish with salt and pepper to taste, adjusting the flavours according to your preference.
Continue cooking the Mutakura for an additional 2-3 minutes, allowing the flavours to meld together.

Serving:
Once the baobab leaves relish is well-cooked and infused with flavours, remove the fry pan from the heat.
Serve the Mutakura hot as a unique and traditional Zimbabwean relish, perfect as a side dish or accompaniment to Sadza (cornmeal porridge) or rice.

Enjoy the delightful taste of Mutakura, a cherished Zimbabwean relish that celebrates the natural bounty of baobab trees and offers a truly authentic culinary experience!

Chikafu Chembudzi - Zimbabwean Goat Meat Stew

Chikafu Chembudzi is a mouthwatering Zimbabwean goat meat stew seasoned with aromatic spices and tomatoes. This hearty and flavourful dish is a celebration of Zimbabwean culinary traditions. Let's explore how to prepare Chikafu Chembudzi step by step:

Ingredients:
1 kg goat meat, cut into bite-sized pieces
1 large onion, finely chopped
2 large tomatoes, chopped
2 tablespoons vegetable oil
2 cloves of garlic, minced
1-inch piece of fresh ginger, grated
1 tablespoon ground paprika
1 tablespoon ground cumin
1 tablespoon ground coriander
1/2 teaspoon ground turmeric
1/2 teaspoon ground black pepper
Salt to taste
Fresh cilantro or parsley, chopped (for garnish)
Cooked Sadza (cornmeal porridge) or rice for serving

Instructions:
Preparing the Goat Meat:
Wash the goat meat pieces thoroughly under running water to remove any debris or impurities.
Cut the goat meat into bite-sized pieces, ensuring they are relatively uniform in size for even cooking.

Sautéing the Aromatics:
In a large, heavy-bottomed pot or Dutch oven, heat the vegetable oil over medium-high heat.
Add the finely chopped onions and sauté until they become translucent, about 2-3 minutes.
Stir in the minced garlic and grated ginger, and cook for an additional minute until aromatic.

Browning the Goat Meat:
Add the goat meat pieces to the pot with the sautéed aromatics.
Brown the meat on all sides to seal in the juices and enhance the flavours. This step adds depth to the stew.

Adding Tomatoes and Spices:
Incorporate the chopped tomatoes into the pot, stirring well to combine with the browned goat meat.
Sprinkle ground paprika, ground cumin, ground coriander, ground turmeric, and ground black pepper over the mixture, coating the meat and tomatoes with the spices.

Simmering the Stew:
Pour enough water into the pot to just cover the goat meat and tomato mixture.
Bring the Chikafu Chembudzi to a gentle simmer, then cover the pot with a lid.

Cooking the Goat Meat:
Let the stew simmer over low to medium heat for about 2 to 2.5 hours (or longer if needed) until the goat meat becomes tender and succulent.

Adjusting Seasoning and Serving:
Taste the stew and add salt if needed, adjusting the seasoning according to your preference.
Once the Chikafu Chembudzi is cooked to perfection, remove the pot from the heat.
Garnish the stew with chopped fresh cilantro or parsley for a burst of freshness.

Serving:
Serve the Chikafu Chembudzi hot, accompanied by Sadza or rice, allowing the rich and flavourful goat meat stew to complement the comforting side dish for a truly satisfying and authentic Zimbabwean meal.

Enjoy the delightful taste of Chikafu Chembudzi, a cherished Zimbabwean dish that showcases the tender and aromatic goat meat stew seasoned with a harmonious blend of spices and tomatoes!

Chingwa - Zimbabwean Baobab Fruit Sauce

Chingwa is a delightful Zimbabwean sauce made from the baobab fruit, known for its unique tangy flavour and high nutritional value. This versatile sauce can be used as a topping for various dishes or incorporated into porridge for a delicious and healthy treat. Let's explore how to prepare Chingwa sauce step by step:

Ingredients:
1 cup baobab fruit pulp (available as dried powder or fresh if possible)
2 tablespoons honey (or sugar as an alternative sweetener)
1 cup water
1 teaspoon ground cinnamon (optional, for added flavour)

Instructions:
Preparing the Baobab Fruit Pulp:
If using dried baobab fruit powder, mix it with 1 cup of water in a bowl, stirring well to create a smooth paste. Let it sit for a few minutes to rehydrate.
If using fresh baobab fruit, remove the pulp from the fruit, discarding any seeds or fibrous parts.

Creating the Chingwa Sauce:
In a saucepan, combine the rehydrated baobab fruit pulp (or fresh pulp) with 1 cup of water.
Add honey (or sugar) to the saucepan, stirring it in to sweeten the sauce.

Simmering the Sauce:
Place the saucepan over medium heat and bring the mixture to a gentle simmer.
Allow the Chingwa sauce to cook for about 5 minutes, stirring occasionally to prevent sticking.

Adjusting Consistency and Flavour:
If the Chingwa sauce seems too thick, you can add a little more water to achieve your desired consistency.

For added flavour, sprinkle ground cinnamon over the sauce, stirring it in to infuse the sauce with a delightful aromatic touch. This step is optional but enhances the overall taste.

Finalizing the Sauce:
Taste the Chingwa sauce and adjust the sweetness level with more honey or sugar if needed, based on your preference.

Serving:
Once the Chingwa sauce has reached your desired consistency and flavour, remove the saucepan from the heat.

Serve the sauce warm or at room temperature, as a delightful topping for pancakes, waffles, ice cream, or yogurt.

Alternatively, you can mix the Chingwa sauce into porridge (e.g., Sadza) to enjoy a nutritious and tangy treat.

Enjoy the unique and tangy flavours of Chingwa, a cherished Zimbabwean sauce made from the baobab fruit, offering a delightful and nutritious addition to various dishes and treats!

Dovi Na Banana - Zimbabwean Peanut Butter Stew with Bananas

Dovi Na Banana is a delightful and unique Zimbabwean dish that combines the rich and creamy flavours of peanut butter stew with the sweetness of ripe bananas. This unexpected pairing creates a delicious and satisfying meal that is sure to delight your taste buds. Let's explore how to prepare Dovi Na Banana step by step:

Ingredients:
500g chicken or beef, cut into bite-sized pieces (vegetarians can use tofu or chickpeas as a substitute)
1 large onion, finely chopped
2 cloves of garlic, minced
1-inch piece of fresh ginger, grated
2 tablespoons vegetable oil
1 cup smooth peanut butter
2 large tomatoes, chopped
2 ripe bananas, sliced
2 cups chicken or vegetable broth (or water)
1 teaspoon ground cumin
1 teaspoon ground coriander
1/2 teaspoon ground turmeric
1/2 teaspoon cayenne pepper (adjust to your preferred level of spiciness)
Salt and pepper to taste
Chopped fresh cilantro or parsley (for garnish)
Cooked Sadza (cornmeal porridge) or rice for serving

Instructions:
Sautéing the Aromatics:
In a large, heavy-bottomed pot or Dutch oven, heat the vegetable oil over medium-high heat.
Add the finely chopped onions and sauté until they become translucent, about 2-3 minutes.
Stir in the minced garlic and grated ginger, and cook for an additional minute until aromatic.

Browning the Chicken or Beef (Optional):
If using chicken or beef, add the meat pieces to the pot with the sautéed aromatics.
Brown the meat on all sides to seal in the juices and enhance the flavours. This step adds depth to the stew. For vegetarian options, skip this step.

Creating the Peanut Butter Sauce:
Reduce the heat to medium-low, then add the smooth peanut butter to the pot.
Stir the peanut butter to soften it and create a smooth and creamy consistency.

Adding Tomatoes and Spices:
Incorporate the chopped tomatoes into the peanut butter sauce, stirring well to combine.
Sprinkle ground cumin, ground coriander, ground turmeric, and cayenne pepper over the sauce, mixing the spices with the tomatoes and peanut butter.

Simmering the Stew:
Pour the chicken or vegetable broth (or water) into the pot, ensuring it covers the sauce and meat (if using).
Bring the Dovi Na Banana to a gentle simmer, then cover the pot with a lid.

Cooking the Stew:
Let the stew simmer over low to medium heat for about 20-30 minutes, allowing the flavours to meld together and the meat (if using) to become tender.

Adding Bananas:
Once the meat (if using) is almost tender, add the sliced ripe bananas to the pot.
Gently stir the bananas into the peanut butter stew, allowing them to infuse their sweetness into the dish.

Adjusting Seasoning and Serving:

Taste the Dovi Na Banana and add salt and pepper to your liking, adjusting the seasoning to your preference.
Continue simmering the stew for an additional 5-10 minutes until the bananas are softened, but not mushy.

Garnishing and Serving:
Once the Dovi Na Banana is cooked to perfection, remove the pot from the heat.

Garnish the stew with chopped fresh cilantro or parsley for a burst of freshness and vibrant colour.

Serve the Dovi Na Banana hot, accompanied by Sadza or rice, allowing the delightful combination of peanut butter stew and sweet bananas to create a truly unique and satisfying Zimbabwean meal.

Enjoy the delicious and unexpected flavours of Dovi Na Banana, a cherished Zimbabwean dish that brings together the creaminess of peanut butter stew and the natural sweetness of ripe bananas for a delightful culinary experience!

Madora - Zimbabwean Flying Ants Delicacy

Madora, the edible flying ants, are a seasonal delicacy cherished in Zimbabwe for their unique taste and nutritional value. This traditional dish is often enjoyed fried as a snack or incorporated into stews for a flavourful and crunchy addition. Let's explore how to prepare Madora step by step:

Note: It is essential to ensure that the flying ants used for this recipe are safe to eat and have not been exposed to any harmful chemicals.

Ingredients:

2 cups fresh or dried flying ants (Madora)
2 tablespoons vegetable oil (for frying, if making fried Madora)
1 large onion, finely chopped
2 large tomatoes, chopped
2 cloves of garlic, minced
1-inch piece of fresh ginger, grated
1 teaspoon ground paprika
1 teaspoon ground cumin
1 teaspoon ground coriander
1/2 teaspoon ground turmeric
Salt and pepper to taste
Fresh cilantro or parsley, chopped (for garnish)
Cooked Sadza (cornmeal porridge) or rice (for serving)

Instructions:

Preparing the Madora:
If using fresh Madora, clean them by removing the wings and legs. Rinse them under cold running water to remove any debris.
If using dried Madora, soak them in water for about 15 minutes to rehydrate them. After rehydration, drain and pat them dry with paper towels.

Frying the Madora (Optional):
If you prefer fried Madora, heat the vegetable oil in a deep fry pan or frying pan over medium-high heat.

Once the oil is hot, carefully add the Madora to the pan in small batches. Fry them until they become crispy and golden brown.
Remove the fried Madora from the oil and place them on a plate lined with paper towels to absorb excess oil.

Sautéing the Aromatics:
In a large fry pan or saucepan, heat a little vegetable oil over medium heat.
Add the finely chopped onions and sauté until they become translucent, about 2-3 minutes.
Stir in the minced garlic and grated ginger, and cook for an additional minute until aromatic.

Creating the Madora Stew (Optional):
If you prefer to make a Madora stew, add the chopped tomatoes to the sautéed aromatics, stirring well to combine.
Sprinkle ground paprika, ground cumin, ground coriander, and ground turmeric over the mixture, mixing the spices with the tomatoes and onions.

Adding the Madora:
Add the prepared Madora (fried or rehydrated) to the saucepan with the sautéed tomatoes and spices.
Gently stir the Madora into the stew, allowing them to absorb the flavours.

Simmering the Stew (Optional):
If making a stew, pour enough water or broth into the saucepan to cover the Madora.
Bring the stew to a gentle simmer, then cover the saucepan with a lid.
Adjusting Seasoning and Serving:

Taste the Madora stew and add salt and pepper to your liking, adjusting the seasoning according to your preference.

Garnishing and Serving:

If making the stew, let it simmer for about 10-15 minutes, allowing the flavours to meld together.

Once the Madora stew is ready, remove the saucepan from the heat.
Garnish the dish with chopped fresh cilantro or parsley for a burst of freshness and colour.
Serve the Madora hot, accompanied by Sadza or rice, allowing this seasonal delicacy to create a unique and flavourful Zimbabwean meal.

Enjoy the distinct and seasonal flavours of Madora, the delightful Zimbabwean flying ants delicacy, whether enjoyed fried as a crunchy snack or as a flavourful addition to a hearty stew!

Maguru/Mudende - Zimbabwean Beef or Goat Tripe Stew

Maguru/Mudende is a flavourful and hearty Zimbabwean dish that features beef or goat tripe cooked until tender in a spicy sauce. This dish is beloved for its rich taste and cultural significance. Let's explore how to prepare Maguru/Mudende stew step by step:

Ingredients:
500g beef or goat tripe, cleaned and cut into small pieces
1 large onion, finely chopped
2 large tomatoes, chopped
2 tablespoons vegetable oil
2 cloves of garlic, minced
1-inch piece of fresh ginger, grated
1 tablespoon ground paprika
1 tablespoon ground cumin
1 tablespoon ground coriander
1/2 teaspoon ground turmeric
1/2 teaspoon cayenne pepper (adjust to your preferred level of spiciness)
Salt and pepper to taste
Fresh cilantro or parsley, chopped (for garnish)
Cooked Sadza (cornmeal porridge) or rice for serving

Instructions:
Preparing the Tripe:
Clean the beef or goat tripe thoroughly under running water to remove any impurities.
Cut the tripe into small pieces, ensuring they are relatively uniform in size for even cooking.

Sautéing the Aromatics:
In a large, heavy-bottomed pot or Dutch oven, heat the vegetable oil over medium-high heat.
Add the finely chopped onions and sauté until they become translucent, about 2-3 minutes.
Stir in the minced garlic and grated ginger, and cook for an additional minute until aromatic.

Browning the Tripe:
Add the tripe pieces to the pot with the sautéed aromatics. Brown the tripe on all sides to enhance the flavours. This step adds depth to the stew.

Adding Tomatoes and Spices:
Incorporate the chopped tomatoes into the pot, stirring well to combine with the browned tripe.
Sprinkle ground paprika, ground cumin, ground coriander, ground turmeric, and cayenne pepper over the mixture, coating the tripe and tomatoes with the spices.

Simmering the Stew:
Pour enough water into the pot to just cover the tripe and tomato mixture.
Bring the Maguru/Mudende stew to a gentle simmer, then cover the pot with a lid.

Cooking the Stew:
Let the stew simmer over low to medium heat for about 2 to 2.5 hours (or longer if needed) until the tripe becomes tender and fully cooked.

Adjusting Seasoning and Serving:
Taste the Maguru/Mudende stew and add salt and pepper to your liking, adjusting the seasoning according to your preference.

Garnishing and Serving:
Once the tripe is tender and infused with flavours, remove the pot from the heat.
Garnish the stew with chopped fresh cilantro or parsley for a burst of freshness and vibrant colour.

Serving:
Serve the Maguru/Mudende stew hot, accompanied by Sadza or rice, allowing the flavourful and tender tripe to meld with the comforting side dish for a truly satisfying and authentic Zimbabwean meal.

Enjoy the rich and spicy flavours of Maguru/Mudende, a cherished Zimbabwean dish that showcases beef or goat tripe cooked until tender in a delightful and aromatic sauce!

Masawu

Masawu, small dried fish, is a flavourful ingredient widely used in Zimbabwean cuisine to add a distinctive taste to various dishes. These dried fish impart a rich umami flavour that enhances stews, sauces, and porridges. Here's how to prepare Masawu and use it to add flavour to a popular Zimbabwean dish called "Sadza neMasawu":

Ingredients:

1 cup Masawu (small dried fish)
2 tablespoons vegetable oil
1 large onion, finely chopped
2 large tomatoes, chopped
2 cloves of garlic, minced
1 teaspoon ground paprika
1 teaspoon ground cumin
1 teaspoon ground coriander
1/2 teaspoon ground turmeric
1/2 teaspoon cayenne pepper (adjust to your preferred level of spiciness)
Salt and pepper to taste
Fresh cilantro or parsley, chopped (for garnish)
Cooked Sadza (cornmeal porridge) or rice for serving

Instructions:

Preparing the Masawu:
Rinse the Masawu under running water to remove any dust or impurities.
Place the dried fish in a bowl of warm water and let them soak for about 15-20 minutes to rehydrate.

Sautéing the Aromatics:
In a large fry pan or saucepan, heat the vegetable oil over medium-high heat.
Add the finely chopped onions and sauté until they become translucent, about 2-3 minutes.
Stir in the minced garlic and cook for an additional minute until aromatic.

Adding Tomatoes and Spices:
Incorporate the chopped tomatoes into the fry pan, stirring well to combine with the sautéed onions.
Sprinkle ground paprika, ground cumin, ground coriander, ground turmeric, and cayenne pepper over the mixture, coating the tomatoes and onions with the spices.

Adding Masawu:
Carefully drain the rehydrated Masawu from the water and add them to the fry pan with the sautéed tomatoes and spices.
Stir the Masawu into the mixture, allowing them to infuse their rich flavour into the sauce.

Simmering and Adjusting Seasoning:
Pour enough water into the fry pan to create a sauce that covers the Masawu and tomato mixture.
Bring the Sadza neMasawu to a gentle simmer, then cover the fry pan with a lid.
Let the dish simmer for about 10-15 minutes, allowing the flavours to meld together.

Seasoning and Garnishing:
Taste the Sadza neMasawu and add salt and pepper to your liking, adjusting the seasoning according to your preference.
If needed, you can add a little more water to achieve your desired consistency for the sauce.

Serving:
Once the Sadza neMasawu is cooked to perfection and the flavours have developed, remove the fry pan from the heat.
Garnish the dish with chopped fresh cilantro or parsley for a burst of freshness and vibrant colour.

Serve Sadza neMasawu hot, alongside Sadza (cornmeal porridge) or rice, allowing the rich umami flavour of the Masawu to enhance this beloved Zimbabwean dish.

Enjoy the delightful flavours of Masawu, the small dried fish that adds a unique and savoury taste to Sadza neMasawu and other dishes in Zimbabwean cuisine!

Chibage Chaunobhobho - Zimbabwean Roasted Corn on the Cob

Chibage Chaunobhobho is a popular street food in Zimbabwe, featuring roasted corn on the cob seasoned with flavourful spices. This delightful snack is enjoyed by locals and visitors alike for its simplicity and delicious taste. Let's learn how to prepare Chibage Chaunobhobho step by step:

Ingredients:

Fresh corn on the cob (as many as desired)
2 tablespoons butter, melted (you can also use oil as a substitute)
1 teaspoon ground paprika
1/2 teaspoon ground cumin
1/2 teaspoon ground coriander
1/4 teaspoon cayenne pepper (adjust to your preferred level of spiciness)
Salt to taste
Fresh lemon wedges (optional, for serving)

Instructions:

Preparing the Corn:
Peel back the husks of the fresh corn but do not remove them completely. Remove the silk threads from the corn.
Rinse the corn under running water to remove any remaining silk or debris.

Soaking the Corn (Optional):
If you prefer, you can soak the corn in cold water for about 30 minutes before roasting. Soaking helps to keep the corn moist during the roasting process.

Preparing the Spice Mix:
In a small bowl, mix the melted butter (or oil) with ground paprika, ground cumin, ground coriander, cayenne pepper, and salt to create the spice mix.

Coating the Corn:
Brush the spice mix evenly over the corn on the cob, ensuring it is fully coated with the flavourful mixture.

Roasting the Corn:
There are two common methods for roasting Chibage Chaunobhobho:
a) On a Grill: Preheat your grill to medium-high heat. Place the spiced corn on the cob directly on the grill grates. Cook the corn, turning occasionally, until it becomes slightly charred and cooked through, about 10-15 minutes.

b) In the Oven: Preheat your oven to 200°C. Wrap each spiced corn on the cob in aluminium foil. Place the wrapped corn on a baking sheet and roast in the oven for about 20-25 minutes, or until the corn is tender.

Serving:
Once the Chibage Chaunobhobho is roasted to perfection, remove the corn from the grill or oven.
Optionally, squeeze fresh lemon juice over the roasted corn for a tangy and refreshing twist.

Enjoying the Street Food Delight:
Serve the Chibage Chaunobhobho hot, savouring the delicious roasted corn on the cob with its delightful blend of spices.

As you enjoy this popular Zimbabwean street food, remember to hold the husks for a convenient and traditional way of handling the delicious treat.

Enjoy the mouth-watering taste of Chibage Chaunobhobho, the Zimbabwean roasted corn on the cob, seasoned with delightful spices for an unforgettable street food experience!

Dochi - Zimbabwean Pumpkin with Groundnut Butter

Dochi is a delectable Zimbabwean dish that features cooked pumpkin infused with the rich flavours of groundnut butter and aromatic spices. This comforting and nutritious dish is loved for its unique combination of sweet and savoury tastes. Let's explore how to prepare Dochi step by step:

Ingredients:

1 medium-sized pumpkin, peeled, seeds removed, and cut into cubes
1/2 cup groundnut butter (peanut butter)
1 large onion, finely chopped
2 large tomatoes, chopped
2 tablespoons vegetable oil
2 cloves of garlic, minced
1 teaspoon ground paprika
1 teaspoon ground cumin
1 teaspoon ground coriander
1/2 teaspoon ground turmeric
1/4 teaspoon cayenne pepper (adjust to your preferred level of spiciness)
Salt and pepper to taste
Fresh cilantro or parsley, chopped (for garnish)
Cooked Sadza (cornmeal porridge) or rice for serving

Instructions:

Preparing the Pumpkin:
Peel the pumpkin using a sharp knife or vegetable peeler.
Cut the pumpkin in half and scoop out the seeds with a spoon.
Cut the pumpkin into bite-sized cubes.

Sautéing the Aromatics:
In a large fry pan or saucepan, heat the vegetable oil over medium-high heat.
Add the finely chopped onions and sauté until they become translucent, about 2-3 minutes.
Stir in the minced garlic and cook for an additional minute until aromatic.

Adding Tomatoes and Spices:
Incorporate the chopped tomatoes into the fry pan, stirring well to combine with the sautéed onions.

Sprinkle ground paprika, ground cumin, ground coriander, ground turmeric, and cayenne pepper over the mixture, coating the tomatoes and onions with the spices.

Cooking the Pumpkin:
Add the pumpkin cubes to the fry pan with the sautéed tomatoes and spices.
Gently stir the pumpkin to combine it with the flavourful mixture.

Simmering the Pumpkin:
Pour enough water into the fry pan to partially cover the pumpkin cubes.
Bring the Dochi to a gentle simmer, then cover the fry pan with a lid.

Infusing with Groundnut Butter:
Spoon the groundnut butter (peanut butter) into the simmering pumpkin mixture.
Stir the groundnut butter into the Dochi, allowing it to melt and coat the pumpkin cubes.

Seasoning and Finalizing:
Season the Dochi with salt and pepper to your liking, adjusting the seasoning according to your preference.
Continue simmering the Dochi for about 10-15 minutes, or until the pumpkin is tender and fully cooked.

Garnishing and Serving:
Once the Dochi is cooked to perfection, remove the fry pan from the heat.
Garnish the dish with chopped fresh cilantro or parsley for a burst of freshness and vibrant colour.

Serving:
Serve the Dochi hot, alongside Sadza or rice, allowing the delightful combination of pumpkin, groundnut butter, and aromatic spices to create a truly satisfying and authentic Zimbabwean meal.

Enjoy the heart-warming taste of Dochi, the Zimbabwean pumpkin dish enriched with groundnut butter and spices, for a comforting and flavourful culinary experience!

Mufushwa - Zimbabwean Fermented Milk Beverage/Dessert

Mufushwa is a delightful Zimbabwean fermented milk beverage, similar to yogurt in texture and taste. This probiotic-rich treat is enjoyed as a refreshing beverage or a creamy dessert. Let's explore how to prepare Mufushwa step by step:

Ingredients:
1 litre fresh milk (cow's milk or goat's milk)
2 tablespoons plain yogurt with live active cultures (as a starter)
2 tablespoons honey or sugar (adjust to your preferred level of sweetness)
1/2 teaspoon vanilla extract (optional, for added flavour)

Instructions:
Heating the Milk (Optional):
Pour the fresh milk into a saucepan or a heatproof container.
Heat the milk over medium heat, stirring occasionally to prevent scorching, until it reaches a temperature of about 85°C.
This step helps to kill any harmful bacteria in the milk and improves the texture of the final product. However, if you prefer raw milk, you can skip this step.

Cooling the Milk:
Allow the heated milk (if using) to cool down to a temperature of around 43°C to 46°C. This temperature range is ideal for the fermentation process.

Mixing the Starter:
In a small bowl, combine the plain yogurt with a small amount of the cooled milk. Stir well to create a smooth mixture.
Add the mixture back into the remaining cooled milk, stirring gently to ensure even distribution of the starter culture.

Fermenting the Milk:
Cover the container with a lid or a clean cloth to prevent any contamination.
Place the container in a warm spot, like a warm kitchen or a closed oven with the light turned on. The warmth helps with the fermentation process.
Allow the milk to ferment for about 6 to 12 hours, or until it thickens and develops a tangy flavour. The fermentation time may vary depending on the ambient temperature and desired tanginess.

Sweetening and Flavouring (Optional):
Once the milk has fermented to your desired taste and texture, add honey or sugar to sweeten the Mufushwa. Stir well until the sweetener is fully dissolved.
For added flavour, you can incorporate vanilla extract, gently stirring it into the fermented milk.

Chilling and Serving:
Transfer the fermented milk (Mufushwa) to the refrigerator to chill for a few hours or overnight. This cooling process helps to thicken the Mufushwa further and enhances its creamy consistency.

Enjoying Mufushwa:
Serve the chilled Mufushwa as a refreshing beverage or a creamy dessert.

You can enjoy it as is or pair it with fresh fruits, nuts, or a drizzle of honey for added sweetness and texture.

Indulge in the delightful taste of Mufushwa, the Zimbabwean fermented milk beverage/dessert, and relish its probiotic goodness and creamy goodness!

Nhingwa - Zimbabwean Roasted Peanuts

Nhingwa is a popular snack in Zimbabwe, consisting of roasted peanuts that are seasoned with flavourful spices. This delightful and easy-to-make treat is perfect for munching on during gatherings, picnics, or as an anytime snack. Let's explore how to prepare Nhingwa step by step:

Ingredients:

2 cups raw peanuts (with shells or without, as preferred)
1 tablespoon vegetable oil
1 teaspoon ground paprika
1 teaspoon ground cumin
1/2 teaspoon ground coriander
1/2 teaspoon cayenne pepper (adjust to your preferred level of spiciness)
Salt to taste

Instructions:

Preparing the Peanuts:
If using peanuts with shells, remove the shells by cracking them open with your fingers. Discard the shells and keep the peanuts.
Rinse the peanuts under running water to remove any dirt or impurities. Pat them dry with a clean kitchen towel.

Preheating the Oven:
Preheat your oven to 180°C.

Seasoning the Peanuts:
In a mixing bowl, toss the peanuts with vegetable oil until they are evenly coated.
Sprinkle ground paprika, ground cumin, ground coriander, cayenne pepper, and salt over the peanuts, mixing well to coat them with the flavourful spices.

Roasting the Peanuts:
Spread the seasoned peanuts in a single layer on a baking sheet lined with baking paper or a silicone baking mat.

Place the baking sheet in the preheated oven and roast the peanuts for about 15-20 minutes, stirring them occasionally to ensure even roasting.

Checking for Doneness:
Keep a close eye on the peanuts as they roast, as they can quickly go from roasted to burnt.
The peanuts are ready when they turn a light golden brown and have a slightly crunchy texture. Be cautious not to over-roast them.

Cooling and Storing:
Once the Nhingwa are roasted to perfection, remove the baking sheet from the oven.
Allow the roasted peanuts to cool completely on the baking sheet before transferring them to an airtight container for storage.

Enjoying Nhingwa:
Serve Nhingwa as a delightful snack during gatherings, parties, picnics, or as an anytime treat.

They can be enjoyed on their own or paired with beverages like tea or soft drinks for a satisfying and flavourful experience.

Prepare a batch of Nhingwa, the Zimbabwean roasted peanuts, and savour the delicious and crunchy taste of this beloved snack that brings joy to many in Zimbabwe!

Gurundoro - Zimbabwean Traditional Popcorn

Gurundoro is a cherished Zimbabwean traditional popcorn snack, loved for its simplicity and deliciousness. It's a perfect treat for movie nights, gatherings, or whenever you're craving a tasty and crunchy snack. Let's explore how to prepare Gurundoro step by step:

Ingredients:
1/2 cup popcorn kernels
2 tablespoons vegetable oil
Salt to taste
Optional toppings: melted butter, powdered seasoning (e.g., paprika, chili powder, garlic powder), grated cheese, or sugar (for sweet popcorn)

Instructions:
Preparing the Popcorn:
In a medium-sized saucepan or a popcorn popper, heat the vegetable oil over medium heat.
Add a few popcorn kernels to the oil and cover the saucepan with a lid.

Testing the Oil:
Once the test kernels pop, it indicates that the oil is hot enough to start popping the rest of the popcorn.

Adding the Popcorn Kernels:
Remove the saucepan from the heat briefly and add the rest of the popcorn kernels to the hot oil.
Cover the saucepan with the lid and let the popcorn kernels sit for about 30 seconds. This step helps the kernels heat evenly.

Popping the Popcorn:
Place the covered saucepan back on the stove over medium heat.
Shake the saucepan occasionally to prevent the popcorn from burning and ensure even popping.

Finishing and Seasoning:
Once the popping slows down significantly (usually after a few minutes), remove the saucepan from the heat.
Let the popcorn sit for a minute or two to ensure all the kernels have popped.

Seasoning the Gurundoro:
While the popcorn is still warm, season it with salt to taste, gently tossing the popcorn to distribute the salt evenly.
If desired, you can add optional toppings like melted butter, powdered seasoning (e.g., paprika, chili powder, garlic powder), grated cheese, or sugar for sweet popcorn. Toss the popcorn gently to coat it with the toppings.

Enjoying Gurundoro:
Serve Gurundoro immediately while it's still warm and crunchy.
Share the delightful Zimbabwean traditional popcorn with family and friends, and savour its deliciousness on various occasions.

Whether it's for a movie night, a gathering, or a simple snack time, Gurundoro offers a delightful and satisfying treat that brings joy to Zimbabwean homes and beyond!

Rupiza, also known as peanut flour

Rupiza, also known as peanut flour or groundnut flour, is a versatile ingredient widely used in Zimbabwean cuisine for its nutty flavour and thickening properties. This finely ground flour is made from roasted and ground peanuts, and it adds a unique taste and texture to various dishes. Let's explore how Rupiza can be used and prepared:

Ingredients:
Raw peanuts (with or without skins)

Instructions:
Roasting the Peanuts (Optional):
Preheat your oven to 180°C.
If using peanuts with skins, spread them in a single layer on a baking sheet.
Roast the peanuts in the preheated oven for about 10-15 minutes until they become aromatic and slightly browned.
Keep an eye on them to avoid burning.
If using peanuts without skins, skip the roasting step.

Removing the Skins (Optional):
If you roasted peanuts with skins, let them cool slightly, then rub them together in your hands or between a kitchen towel to remove the skins. Discard the skins.

Grinding the Peanuts:
Once the peanuts are roasted and/or skins removed, place them in a food processor or a high-powered blender.
Grind the peanuts until they reach a fine, powdery consistency. You can also leave them slightly coarse if you prefer.

Sieving (Optional):
To achieve a smoother texture, you can pass the ground peanuts through a fine-mesh sieve or strainer to remove any larger pieces or remaining skin particles.

Storing Rupiza:
Transfer the groundnut flour (Rupiza) to an airtight container. Store it in a cool, dry place away from direct sunlight. Properly stored, Rupiza can last for several months.

Using Rupiza in Various Dishes:
Thickening Stews and Sauces:
Rupiza is commonly used as a thickener in Zimbabwean stews and sauces. To use it, mix a small amount of Rupiza with water to create a smooth paste, then add it to the simmering stew or sauce. Stir well to incorporate, and the Rupiza will help thicken the dish and add a nutty flavour.

Baking and Cooking:
Rupiza can be used as an alternative flour in baking recipes, adding a nutty taste to cookies, muffins, and other baked goods.
It can also be sprinkled over vegetables, salads, or roasted meats to add a nutty crunch.

Rupiza Porridge:
To make a hearty Rupiza porridge, combine the groundnut flour with water or milk in a saucepan. Cook it over medium heat while stirring continuously until it thickens to your desired consistency. Sweeten with sugar or honey, and optionally, add spices like cinnamon for extra flavour.

Rupiza is a wonderful and versatile ingredient that brings a distinct nutty taste and thickening properties to various dishes in Zimbabwean cuisine. Its unique flavour and texture make it a beloved addition to many traditional recipes.

Bohobe - Zimbabwean Sorghum and Maize Drink

Bohobe is a traditional Zimbabwean drink made from a combination of sorghum and maize. It is often consumed at special occasions, gatherings, and celebrations. This nutritious and flavourful drink is not only refreshing but also holds cultural significance. Let's explore how to prepare Bohobe step by step:

Ingredients:

1 cup sorghum grains
1 cup maize (corn) kernels
8 cups water
1/2 cup sugar (adjust to your preferred level of sweetness)
1 teaspoon vanilla extract (optional, for added flavour)
A pinch of salt
Milk or coconut milk (optional, for a creamier version)

Instructions:

Preparing the Sorghum and Maize:
Rinse the sorghum grains and maize kernels under running water to remove any debris.
In a bowl, soak the sorghum and maize in water overnight or for at least 6-8 hours. This soaking process helps soften the grains and aids in the blending process.

Blending the Grains:
After soaking, drain the water from the sorghum and maize.
In a blender or food processor, add the soaked sorghum and maize along with 4 cups of water.
Blend the mixture until you achieve a smooth and fine consistency.

Straining the Mixture:
Place a fine-mesh sieve or a cheesecloth over a large bowl.
Pour the blended sorghum and maize mixture through the sieve or cheesecloth to separate the liquid from the solid particles.

Use a spoon or spatula to press and extract as much liquid as possible from the mixture. This liquid is your Bohobe drink.

Boiling the Bohobe:
In a large saucepan, combine the extracted Bohobe liquid with the remaining 4 cups of water.
Add sugar and a pinch of salt to the mixture.
Optionally, add vanilla extract for extra flavour.

Cooking the Bohobe:
Place the saucepan on the stove over medium heat.
Bring the Bohobe mixture to a gentle boil, stirring occasionally to dissolve the sugar and incorporate the flavours.
Let the Bohobe simmer for about 10-15 minutes, allowing it to thicken slightly.

Serving Bohobe:
Once the Bohobe has simmered to your desired consistency, remove the saucepan from the heat.
You can serve Bohobe warm or chilled, depending on your preference.
Optionally, for a creamier version, add a splash of milk or coconut milk before serving.

Enjoying Bohobe:
Serve Bohobe in cups or glasses, and savour the wholesome and culturally significant Zimbabwean drink, perfect for special occasions and celebrations.

Bohobe is a delightful and nourishing drink that combines the goodness of sorghum and maize, making it a cherished part of Zimbabwean traditions and gatherings. Enjoy this refreshing beverage as you celebrate special moments with loved ones.

Chikanda, also known as African Polony

Chikanda, also known as African Polony or African Sausage, is a unique dessert enjoyed in some parts of Southern and Central Africa, including Zimbabwe. It is made from groundnuts (peanuts) and the tubers of certain wild orchid species. This sweet and chewy dessert holds cultural significance and is often associated with traditional and festive occasions. It is important to note that the use of wild orchid tubers has raised concerns about sustainability and conservation, and it is essential to ensure responsible sourcing or consider alternative ingredients.

Please be advised that the use of wild orchid tubers should only be done sustainably and legally, following local regulations and considering the impact on the environment. To ensure a sustainable and ethical preparation of Chikanda, it is best to use an alternative ingredient like cassava flour or sweet potato as a substitute for wild orchid tubers. Here's a recipe for Chikanda using cassava flour as a substitute:

Ingredients:

1 cup groundnuts (peanuts), roasted and finely ground
1 cup cassava flour (or sweet potato flour) - as a substitute for wild orchid tubers
1/2 cup sugar or honey (adjust to your preferred level of sweetness)
1/2 cup water
1/2 teaspoon ground cinnamon (optional, for added flavour)
Banana leaves or baking paper (for wrapping)

Instructions:

Preparing the Groundnuts:
Roast the groundnuts in a dry pan over medium heat until they are lightly browned and aromatic.
Once roasted, allow the groundnuts to cool down, then grind them into a fine powder using a food processor or grinder.

Mixing the Ingredients:
In a mixing bowl, combine the ground roasted groundnuts with cassava flour (or sweet potato flour) to serve as a substitute for wild orchid tubers.
Add sugar or honey to the mixture, adjusting the sweetness according to your preference.
If desired, add ground cinnamon to enhance the flavour.

Adding Water:
Gradually add water to the mixture while stirring continuously until it forms a dough-like consistency. The dough should hold together without being too sticky.

Shaping the Chikanda:
Take small portions of the dough and shape them into round or sausage-like pieces, about the size of small cookies or energy balls.

Wrapping the Chikanda:
Place each Chikanda piece onto a banana leaf or a piece of baking paper.
Wrap the Chikanda tightly in the leaf or paper, securing it to hold its shape.

Chilling and Setting:
Place the wrapped Chikanda in the refrigerator for at least 1-2 hours to firm up and set.

Serving Chikanda:
Once chilled and set, unwrap the Chikanda and serve it as a unique and sweet dessert.

Enjoy the delightful taste of Chikanda, a dessert with cultural significance, while considering the use of sustainable and ethical ingredients.

Chakalaka

Chakalaka is a popular and spicy vegetable relish that originates from South Africa and is widely enjoyed across the region, including Zimbabwe. This flavourful condiment adds a burst of vibrant colours and bold taste to various dishes, making it a versatile accompaniment in Zimbabwean cuisine. Let's explore how to prepare Chakalaka step by step:

Ingredients:

2 tablespoons vegetable oil
1 large onion, finely chopped
2 cloves of garlic, minced
1-2 hot chili peppers (e.g., jalapeno or serrano), finely chopped (adjust to your preferred level of spiciness)
1 large carrot, grated
1 large red capsicum, diced
1 large green capsicum, diced
1 can (400g) baked beans in tomato sauce (or any canned beans of your choice)
1 can (400g) chopped tomatoes
1 teaspoon ground cumin
1 teaspoon ground coriander
1 teaspoon paprika
1/2 teaspoon ground turmeric
Salt and pepper to taste
Fresh cilantro or parsley, chopped (for garnish)

Instructions:
Sautéing the Aromatics:
In a large saucepan or fry pan, heat the vegetable oil over medium-high heat.
Add the finely chopped onions and sauté until they become translucent, about 2-3 minutes.
Stir in the minced garlic and chopped hot chili peppers, and continue cooking for an additional minute until aromatic.

Adding Vegetables:
Add the grated carrot, diced red capsicum, and diced green capsicum to the fry pan.
Sauté the vegetables for about 5 minutes, or until they start to soften.

Spices and Tomatoes:
Sprinkle ground cumin, ground coriander, paprika, and ground turmeric over the sautéed vegetables.
Stir the spices into the mixture to coat the vegetables evenly.
Pour in the canned chopped tomatoes (with their juice) and canned baked beans in tomato sauce.

Simmering Chakalaka:
Reduce the heat to medium-low and let the Chakalaka simmer for about 15-20 minutes, stirring occasionally. The flavours will meld together, and the sauce will thicken slightly.

Adjusting Seasoning:
Taste the Chakalaka and add salt and pepper according to your preference, adjusting the seasoning as needed to suit your taste.

Garnishing:
Once the Chakalaka is cooked to perfection, remove the fry pan from the heat.
Garnish the dish with freshly chopped cilantro or parsley for a burst of freshness and vibrant colours.

Serving Chakalaka:
Serve Chakalaka hot or at room temperature as a spicy vegetable relish that complements various dishes.

It pairs exceptionally well with grilled meats, roasted vegetables, rice, bread, or as a flavourful topping for Sadza (cornmeal porridge).

Enjoy the bold and spicy flavours of Chakalaka, the Zimbabwean vegetable relish that brings an exciting kick to your favourite dishes!

Chingondora

Chingondora is a delicious Zimbabwean dish made from pumpkin flowers and groundnut butter (peanut butter). It is a unique and flavourful combination of ingredients that creates a delightful and nutritious meal. Pumpkin flowers, also known as pumpkin blossoms or pumpkin blooms, are edible and have a slightly sweet taste, making them a delightful addition to this dish. Let's explore how to prepare Chingondora step by step:

Ingredients:
2 cups pumpkin flowers (pumpkin blossoms), washed and trimmed
1/2 cup groundnut butter (peanut butter)
1 large onion, finely chopped
2 large tomatoes, chopped
2 tablespoons vegetable oil
2 cloves of garlic, minced
1 teaspoon ground paprika
1 teaspoon ground cumin
1/2 teaspoon ground coriander
1/4 teaspoon cayenne pepper (adjust to your preferred level of spiciness)
Salt to taste

Instructions:
Preparing the Pumpkin Flowers:
Wash the pumpkin flowers thoroughly under running water to remove any dirt or debris.
Trim off the stems and any tough parts, leaving only the tender parts of the flowers.

Sautéing the Aromatics:
In a large fry pan or saucepan, heat the vegetable oil over medium-high heat.
Add the finely chopped onions and sauté until they become translucent, about 2-3 minutes.
Stir in the minced garlic and cook for an additional minute until aromatic.

Adding Tomatoes and Spices:
Incorporate the chopped tomatoes into the fry pan with the sautéed onions.
Sprinkle ground paprika, ground cumin, ground coriander, and cayenne pepper over the mixture, coating the tomatoes and onions with the spices.

Cooking the Pumpkin Flowers:
Add the washed and trimmed pumpkin flowers to the fry pan with the sautéed tomatoes and spices.
Gently stir the pumpkin flowers to combine them with the flavourful mixture.

Infusing with Groundnut Butter:
Spoon the groundnut butter (peanut butter) into the fry pan with the pumpkin flowers, tomatoes, and spices.
Add a small amount of water to the fry pan to create a smooth sauce and help the groundnut butter blend with the other ingredients.

Seasoning and Simmering:
Season the Chingondora with salt to your liking, adjusting the seasoning according to your preference.
Let the Chingondora simmer for about 10-15 minutes, stirring occasionally, until the pumpkin flowers are tender and fully cooked.

Serving Chingondora:
Once the Chingondora is cooked to perfection, remove the fry pan from the heat.

Serve the Chingondora hot, alongside Sadza (cornmeal porridge) or rice, for a delightful and nutritious Zimbabwean meal.

Enjoy the delectable taste of Chingondora, the Zimbabwean dish made from pumpkin flowers and groundnut butter, combining the earthy flavours of the pumpkin flowers with the richness of groundnut butter for a truly satisfying culinary experience!

Mapopo Candy

Mapopo Candy is a delightful Zimbabwean treat made from candied or dried guava fruit. This sweet and chewy candy captures the natural flavours of guava, creating a delicious and tropical snack that is loved by many. Here's how you can make Mapopo Candy at home:

Ingredients:
Ripe guava fruits
Sugar
Water

Instructions:
Preparing the Guava:
Choose ripe guava fruits that are fragrant and slightly soft to the touch. Wash the guavas thoroughly under running water to remove any dirt or impurities.

Peeling and Deseeding:
Peel the guava fruits and remove any blemishes or dark spots on the skin.
Cut the guavas in half and scoop out the seeds using a spoon. Discard the seeds.

Slicing the Guava:
Slice the guava fruits into thin, uniform pieces. You can cut them into rounds or strips, depending on your preference.

Preparing the Syrup:
In a saucepan, combine equal parts of sugar and water. For example, if you use 1 cup of sugar, add 1 cup of water.

Boiling the Syrup:
Heat the sugar-water mixture over medium heat, stirring until the sugar completely dissolves.
Bring the syrup to a gentle boil.

Candying the Guava:
Add the sliced guava pieces to the boiling syrup, making sure they are fully submerged in the liquid.
Reduce the heat to low and let the guava slices simmer in the syrup for about 15-20 minutes, or until they become translucent and tender.

Drying the Guava:
Using a slotted spoon, remove the candied guava slices from the syrup, allowing any excess syrup to drip off.
Place the candied guava slices on a wire rack or a baking-lined baking sheet to dry. Make sure they are evenly spaced to prevent sticking.

Drying Options:
You can let the candied guava slices air-dry at room temperature for a few hours until they become chewy and slightly tacky.
Alternatively, you can dry them in a food dehydrator or in a low-temperature oven around 50°C for a quicker drying process.

Storing Mapopo Candy:
Once the candied guava slices are completely dry, store them in an airtight container to maintain their freshness and chewy texture.

Enjoy the delicious and tropical flavours of Mapopo Candy, the candied or dried guava fruit that brings a taste of Zimbabwe to your snacking experience!

Dobi, also known as Chibage

Dobi, also known as Chibage, is a popular traditional Zimbabwean leafy green vegetable that is similar to spinach. It is a nutritious and versatile vegetable that is widely enjoyed in Zimbabwean cuisine. Dobi is known for its earthy flavour and tender leaves, making it a delightful addition to various dishes. Here's a simple recipe on how to prepare Dobi:

Ingredients:
1 bunch of Dobi (Chibage) greens
1 tablespoon vegetable oil
1 large onion, finely chopped
2 cloves of garlic, minced
1-2 hot chili peppers (e.g., jalapeno or serrano), finely chopped (optional, adjust to your preferred level of spiciness)
Salt and pepper to taste
Lemon juice (optional, for added tanginess)

Instructions:
Preparing the Dobi Greens:
Wash the Dobi greens thoroughly under running water to remove any dirt or debris.
Trim off any tough stems and separate the leaves.

Blanching the Dobi:
Bring a large pot of water to a boil.
Add the Dobi leaves to the boiling water and blanch them for about 1-2 minutes, or until they become bright green and slightly wilted.

Draining and Cooling:
Using a slotted spoon or a strainer, remove the blanched Dobi leaves from the boiling water and immediately transfer them to a bowl of ice-cold water. This helps stop the cooking process and preserves their vibrant green colour.

Sautéing the Aromatics:
In a large fry pan or pan, heat the vegetable oil over medium-high heat.
Add the finely chopped onions and sauté until they become translucent, about 2-3 minutes.
Stir in the minced garlic and chopped hot chili peppers (if using) and continue cooking for an additional minute until aromatic.

Adding the Dobi Greens:
Drain the blanched Dobi leaves from the cold water and squeeze out any excess water.
Add the Dobi greens to the fry pan with the sautéed onions, garlic, and chili peppers.

Seasoning and Cooking:
Season the Dobi greens with salt and pepper to your liking.
Gently toss the greens in the fry pan, making sure they are coated with the aromatic mixture.
Cook the Dobi greens for about 3-5 minutes, or until they are tender and fully cooked.

Optional Tanginess:
For added tanginess, you can drizzle some fresh lemon juice over the cooked Dobi greens before serving.

Serving Dobi:
Serve the Dobi greens as a nutritious and flavourful side dish alongside your favourite main courses, such as Sadza (cornmeal porridge) and grilled meats.

Enjoy the delectable taste of Dobi, the traditional Zimbabwean greens that bring a delightful burst of flavour and nutrition to your mealtime!

Chikwata

Chikwata is a delicious sweet and sour sauce made from tamarind fruit, commonly used as a dip or marinade in Zimbabwean cuisine. Tamarind provides a unique tangy flavour that perfectly complements a variety of dishes, adding depth and complexity to the flavours. This versatile sauce can be served with grilled meats, vegetables, or used as a marinade to enhance the taste of various ingredients. Here's how to prepare Chikwata sauce:

Ingredients:

1 cup tamarind pulp (from tamarind fruit)
1 cup hot water
2 tablespoons brown sugar (adjust to your preferred level of sweetness)
1 tablespoon soy sauce
1 tablespoon vegetable oil
1 clove of garlic, minced
1 teaspoon grated ginger
1/2 teaspoon red pepper flakes (optional, for added spiciness)
Salt to taste

Instructions:

Preparing the Tamarind Pulp:
Break the tamarind pulp into small pieces and place it in a bowl.
Pour the hot water over the tamarind pulp, allowing it to soak and soften for about 15-20 minutes.

Extracting Tamarind Juice:
Once the tamarind pulp has softened, use your fingers to gently break it apart, separating the seeds and fibres from the pulp.
Strain the tamarind pulp through a fine-mesh sieve into another bowl, pressing it with a spoon to extract the tamarind juice. Discard the seeds and fibres.

Making the Chikwata Sauce:
In a saucepan, heat the vegetable oil over medium heat. Add the minced garlic and grated ginger to the hot oil, sautéing them until fragrant, about 1-2 minutes.

Adding Tamarind Juice and Seasonings:
Pour the extracted tamarind juice into the saucepan with the sautéed garlic and ginger.
Stir in the brown sugar, soy sauce, and red pepper flakes (if using) into the tamarind mixture.

Simmering Chikwata:
Bring the sauce to a gentle simmer, allowing it to cook for about 5-7 minutes, stirring occasionally to let the flavours meld together.
Taste the Chikwata sauce and adjust the sweetness and saltiness to your liking.

Thickening the Sauce (Optional):
If you prefer a thicker consistency, you can let the Chikwata sauce simmer for a few more minutes until it reaches your desired thickness. Keep in mind that the sauce will thicken further as it cools.

Cooling and Serving:
Once the Chikwata sauce is cooked to your satisfaction, remove the saucepan from the heat and let it cool slightly.

Transfer the Chikwata sauce to a serving bowl and serve it as a delicious dip or marinade alongside your favourite dishes.

Enjoy the delightful sweet and sour flavours of Chikwata, the Zimbabwean tamarind sauce, and savour its versatile taste that complements various culinary creations!